AMISH
Baking

AMISH

Baking

Traditional Recipes for Bread, Cookies, Cakes, and Pies

*from the
editors of Good Books*

Good Books

New York, New York

10 9 8 7

Library of Congress Cataloging-in-Publication Data is available on file.

Cover design by Daniel Brount
Cover and interior photos courtesy of Getty Images

Print ISBN: 978-1-68099-598-5

Printed in China

CONTENTS

AN INTRODUCTION TO THE AMISH AND THEIR FOOD

The Amish have captured the interest of the modern world because of their quaint clothing, homes, and buggies, their striking quilts, their lusty food. These people prefer to be regarded as a community of faith who deliberately seek to live in a way that honors God and the creation. They purposely refuse many conveniences to better foster their life together; they choose to live close to the land in an effort to care for their families and the earth.

Who Are These People?

The Amish are a Christian group who trace their beginnings to the time of the Protestant Reformation in 16th century Europe.

In 1525 a group of believers parted company with the established state church for a variety of reasons. Among them was the conviction that one must voluntarily become a follower of Christ, and that that deliberate decision will be reflected in all of one's life. Therefore, baptism must symbolize that choice. The movement was nicknamed "Anabaptists," meaning rebaptism, since the believers wanted to be baptized again as adults.

Eventually the group were called Mennonites after Menno Simons, one of their leaders who had formerly been a Roman Catholic priest. Over the years these people grew into a strong faith community, concerned with the nurture and discipline of each other.

Basic to their beliefs was a conviction that if one was a faithful follower of Christ's, one's behavior would clearly distinguish one from the larger world. These people saw themselves as separated unto God because of their values of love, forgiveness, and peace. Because they were misunderstood and because they appeared to be a threat to the established church and government, the people were often persecuted and many became refugees.

In 1693, a magnetic young Mennonite leader believed that the church was losing some of its purity and that it was beginning to compromise with the world. And so he and a group who agreed with him left the Mennonites and formed a separate fellowship. They were called Amish, after their leader, Jacob Amman. Today the Amish identify themselves as the most conservative group of Mennonites.

The movement which Amman began reached into Switzerland, Alsace, and the Palatinate area of Germany. As early as 1727 Amish families began to resettle in North America, where they found farmland, space to live as neighbors to each other, and a climate that nurtured their growth as a church family with a distinctive lifestyle.

The tiny communities struggled to survive in the early years. As was true for other pioneers, the Amish invested most of their time and energy in clearing the land, establishing their homesteads, and getting along with the Native Americans. Most of those who arrived from the 1720s through the mid-1760s settled in eastern Pennsylvania, yet they did not live in sequestered communities.

Frequently they had neighbors who were not Amish. With that came the opportunity for interchange with folks from the larger world. Nor was the Amish church as defined in terms of distinctive practices nor as organized under recognized leaders as it became following the American Revolution. That event crystallized many of the convictions these people held and united them in their refusal to join the War, since they were (and remain today) conscientious objectors.

The Amish intend to give their primary attention and energy to being faithful disciples of the teachings of Jesus Christ. They believe they can do that best as members of a community who together share that desire. Consequently they have tried to withstand acculturation into the "worldly" society surrounding them. They have remained close to the land, preferring to farm if at all possible. They believe hard work is honorable, that church and family provide one's primary identity. Their ideal in life is not to pursue careers that lead to prosperity and prestige, but to become responsible and contributing members to their faith community.

The Amish have changed throughout their nearly 300 years of history. Their intent, however, is to be deliberate about change, to manage it carefully so that it does not erode their convictions.

The Amish continue to grow. Today they live in 20 states and one Canadian province, totaling about 100,000 adults and children. There are twice as many Amish persons today as there were only 20 years ago. They are a living and dynamic people.

What Is Their Food Tradition in the New World?

Because they are highly disciplined, the Amish are often perceived as being grim, austere folks who live as ascetics. They do live ordered lives and, in general, are restrained in their outward expression. But in two particular areas they have exercised color—in their quilts and in their food! In both areas they distinguished themselves only after becoming established in North America. By the mid-1850s and during the next several decades a food tradition evolved that included an amalgam of dishes from a variety of sources: they brought their own cultural taste preferences from Switzerland and Germany; that affected what they copied and adapted from the diets of their English and Native American neighbors; the geography and climate in the area of the New World where they made their homes also shaped their eating. In those ways, however, they were little different from the other German folk who settled in William Penn's colony.

How, then, did the Amish develop and retain a food tradition that is identifiable? With their sustained rural base, the Amish have continued a productive relationship with their gardens and fields. With their large extended families, they have not only been able to convey the love of certain dishes to their children, but they have also been able to show their daughters how to make those specialties, many of which are learned best by "feel" than by reading a cookbook. In addition, their active community life supports the continuation of a food tradition—at gathered times, favorite dishes appear, undergirding the event, whether it be a school picnic, a funeral, or sisters' day.

Several principles prevail among these people with as much strength now as they did when the first Amish built their homestead in Pennsylvania: To waste is to destroy God's gift. To be slack,

work-wise, is to be disrespectful of time and resources. To go hungry is to ignore the bounty of the earth (furthermore, there is no reason that eating shouldn't be a pleasure!).

The Amish are hard workers whose efforts on the land have been rewarded with fruitful fields and gardens. And so they have eaten well. In fact, their land has been so productive that Amish cooks have undertaken massive "pickling" operations, preserving the excess from their gardens in sweet and sour syrups. Likely one amazed guest, who sat at the table of an Amish cook or who witnessed her well-stocked canning shelves, began the tale of "seven sweets and seven sours." That exaggeration of what is typically served has a bit of truth at its core—hard work has its payoff and all food is made to be enjoyed.

Desserts are eaten daily in most Amish homes. But multiple desserts at one meal are generally eaten only when there is company. Thus the story of manifold pastries available at every meal has only a shade of truth in it.

What Does This Cookbook Contain?

This cookbook is a collection of those dishes that go back as far as 80-year-old members of the Amish church can recall or discover in hand-written "cookbooks" which belong to their mothers, and that are still prepared today, either in the old-fashioned way or by an adapted method. These foods are ones that were—and still are —eaten (perhaps now in a modified form), in eastern Pennsylvania, most often in the Lancaster area. It was in that general community that the first Amish settlements took root and grew. Although Lancaster gave birth to many daughter colonies, it is today the second-largest Amish community (Holmes County, Ohio, is the largest).

Typically those handwritten and food-spattered cookbooks included only ingredients without any, or with only minimal, reference to procedures. Furthermore, the measurements were far from precise! Most Amish folks recall that their mothers seldom consulted a cookbook anyway. Experience kept their skills polished. In keeping with the Amish tradition of living as extended families, an elderly mother or aunt was usually nearby to offer help.

Amish Baking contains old recipes, but they are written to be understood and used by those without the benefit of these people's history or the presence of an experienced cook.

Note: Throughout the book, pronoun references to the cook in Amish homes are consistently of the feminine gender. This was done deliberately, since in Amish society, roles are clearly defined. Women are solely responsible for food preparation, apart from butchering and related processes such as drying and smoking, certain gardening chores, and making apple or pear butter. A man who carries primary responsibilities in the kitchen is a rare exception.

Breads

Bread baking is on its way back, at least among many Amish women today. When home-delivered, "bought" bread became available, the Amish were as eager customers for it as were their non-Amish neighbors. The reason? "In the outdoor bake ovens, as well as in the ovens of ranges, you couldn't control the temperature," recalls one Amish cook. "What's more, the flour wasn't as good as it is today. And the yeast certainly wasn't!"

Immediately after its baking, the bread from bake ovens and ranges was tasty and pleasing in its texture. "But they used a lot of flour, and it got dry pretty quickly. I work with a lot stickier dough than they used to," comments an Amish woman in her mid-thirties. She learned to bake bread from her grandmother-in-law because her mother bought their family's bread.

Few outdoor bake ovens remain today. Those early structures were built with their own chimneys and drafts and were often covered with a roof. Their size made possible the baking of many loaves of bread at once, an efficiency measure for a cook with many children and frequently a farmhand or two to feed. It also meant that baking needed to be done only once a week, usually on Friday, so that there was fresh bread for the weekend. The bread that remained until the next baking day, however, was no one's favorite!

In the late 1800s, some bake ovens were built with their openings in the washhouses that were attached to the farmhouses. Others were part of the farms' shop buildings where tools were kept. Those few people who recall the presence of bake ovens remember that they were used in a limited way, or not at all. "We did our baking for church in the bake oven," a woman born in the mid-1940s explained. (The fact that so many loaves could be baked at once, and that they were eaten within a day of their baking, made the use of the bake oven acceptable for that function.) "After the oven had cooled down somewhat, Mother would put field corn in there on racks to dry (in preparation for cornmeal) and also snitz for pies."

Another woman, born in 1904, remembers that a bake oven stood on her grandparents' farm, but was not used within her memory. "I know that when I was a child we would open the gate in our front yard for the baker who would give each of us a cookie! It was so much work to bake bread then. I remember the 5¢ loaf. It was no wonder people didn't make their own!"

Furthermore, during the summertime when bread didn't keep as well because of the heat, and when there were more helpers around because of the extra fieldwork, baking needed to be done twice a week. That task, even using the more modern range, was a steamy chore. There was simply little incentive for home breadbaking.

In the early to mid-1950s, numbers of Amish women began making their own bread. An Amish historian believes that change may have been related to the development of "wrapped bought bread." The loaves he remembers his mother buying when he was a child were made with yeast, were unsliced, and were baked fast to the loaves on either side of it. But along with the packaging of bread some years later came the use of "unusual ingredients" instead of yeast. That change, along with the availability of improved yeast for home baking (no more trips to the old neighbor woman who grew and kept the homemade yeast!), more evenly textured flour, and stoves with refined calibration, triggered an interest in breadbaking among many Amish cooks.

The women may have been ready to swing into baking bread, but the men were not ready to eat it. Recalls one cook, "When we started baking bread we had to train the men to eat something other than bought white bread! We had all learned that a sandwich with homemade bread at school was not something we appreciated."

Another remembers, "When we were first married I wanted to bake all our own bread. But my husband said, 'Nothin' doin'!' My dad always preferred bought bread, too,"

In time the Amish cooks who wanted to bake yeast breads have proven their skill. Their families' tastes have been converted.

WHITE BREAD

Makes 2 large or 3 medium loaves.

Ingredients:

1 package yeast
1 tsp. sugar
2½ cups lukewarm water, divided
1¼ tsp. salt
⅓ cup sugar
1¾ Tbsp. shortening
7–8 cups flour

Instructions:

1. Dissolve the yeast and sugar in ½ cup lukewarm water. Mix 2 cups water, salt, sugar, and shortening. Then add the yeast mixture and, gradually, the flour.

2. Knead until smooth and elastic. Place in a greased bowl, cover and set in a warm place to rise until double.

3. Punch down. Let rise again. Put in two large loaf pans or three medium ones. Let rise until double again. Bake at 350°F for ½ hour.

Recipe Notes: The Old Order Amish meet in homes for their Sunday-morning services. The hosting family, with the assistance of neighbors and extended family, prepares a lunch for all who have attended.

An Amish mother of nine grown children explains, "Now for church we use homemade bread. Years ago we bought it. But it's cheaper to make our own—and better. We help each other so that whoever has church doesn't need to make it all."

WHOLE WHEAT BREAD

Makes 4 loaves.

Ingredients:

2 packages dry yeast
4 cups warm water
½ cup margarine or butter, softened
¼ cup molasses
½ cup honey
2 tsp. salt
6 cups whole wheat flour
4 cups white flour

Instructions:

1. Dissolve yeast in warm water.

2. Combine margarine, molasses, honey, and salt and mix well. Add yeast mixture.

3. Gradually add flour. Turn dough onto floured board and knead until smooth, about 7–10 minutes.

4. Place in greased bowl and let rise until double. Punch down. Let dough rest a few minutes.

5. Shape into 4 loaves. Place in greased bread pans and let rise about 1 hour.

6. Bake at 375°F for 35–40 minutes.

Recipe Notes: Reflecting the more health-conscious attitude of many Amish cooks today, this recipe uses honey in place of sugar and whole wheat flour instead of all white flour.

YEAST BUNS

Makes 3–3½ dozen rolls.

Ingredients:

3 packages dry yeast
1 cup lukewarm water
2 cups milk
½ cup lard or vegetable oil
½ cup sugar
7–8 cups flour, divided
1 Tbsp. salt

Instructions:

1. Dissolve the yeast in the lukewarm water. Set aside. Scald milk and add the lard and sugar to it. Let cool to lukewarm, then add yeast mixture to it.

2. Beat in 3½–4 cups flour. Let rest in warm place for ½ hour.

3. Beat in salt and remaining flour. Knead on lightly floured surface until the dough is no longer sticky. Let rise until double in bulk.

4. Punch down, then form into balls the size of a large walnut. Place in a greased baking pan and let rise again until nearly double.

5. Bake at 400°F for 15–20 minutes or until golden brown.

POTATO BREAD

Makes 3 loaves.

Ingredients:
3½ cups milk
6 Tbsp. sugar
6 Tbsp. butter
2 tsp. salt
½ cup mashed potatoes
2 packages dry yeast
½ cup lukewarm water
3 cups whole wheat flour
7–8 cups white flour, divided

Instructions:

1. Scald milk. Add sugar, butter, salt, and mashed potatoes. Cool to lukewarm.

2. Meanwhile, dissolve yeast in water. Add to cooled milk mixture.

3. Add whole wheat flour and 1 cup white flour. Beat 2 minutes with mixer. Stir in 6–7 more cups flour until dough leaves sides of bowl.

4. Turn onto lightly floured surface. Knead gently until dough forms a smooth ball. Place in greased bowl. Turn once to grease top of dough. Cover and let rise in a warm place away from drafts until doubled, 1½–2 hours. Punch down and let rise again until double.

5. Turn onto floured surface and divide dough into 3 equal parts. Cover and let rest 10 minutes.

6. Form into 3 loaves and place in greased bread pans.

7. Bake at 350°F for 40–45 minutes. Remove from pans and place on rack to cool.

CORN BREAD

Makes one 8-inch pan.

Ingredients:
¾ cup roasted yellow cornmeal
I cup flour
¼ cup sugar
¾ tsp. salt
3½ tsp. baking powder
I cup milk
I egg, beaten
¼ cup vegetable oil or lard, melted

Instructions:

1. Stir together dry ingredients.

2. Mix liquid ingredients together. Make a well in the dry ingredients, then add liquid all at once. Beat thoroughly.

3. Pour into greased 8-inch square cake pan or cast-iron pan. Bake at 400°F for 25–30 minutes. Serve warm.

Recipe Notes: "Mother made a shortcake—not a yeast bread—with cornmeal. We ate it hot and always with canned sour cherries for our snack meal or Saturday dinnertime."

POTATO BUNS AND DOUGHNUTS

Makes about 3 dozen.

Ingredients:

1 cup sugar
1 cup mashed potatoes
½ cup lard
3 eggs, beaten
1½ tsp. salt
1½–2 packs yeast
1 cup warm water
5 cups flour

Instructions:

1. Combine the sugar, potatoes, lard, eggs, and salt. Mix together well.

2. Dissolve the yeast in 1 cup warm water; then add that to the above mixture.

3. Stir in about 3 cups of flour. Add the remaining 2 cups flour while kneading. Knead until the dough is no longer sticky but moist.

4. Let rise until doubled.

Recipe Notes: Someone learned that adding mashed potatoes to the dough for rolls and doughnuts created an appetizing softness in the finished delicacy. Now the Amish baker makes more mashed potatoes than she believes her family can eat at the main meal—"planned" leftovers, with a pleasing destination!

For Potato Buns:

1. Roll out dough to a thickness of ¾ inch–1 inch. Cut into bun shapes with a jar or doughnut cutter (or a cutter shaped like a clover leaf or crescent) and put on greased cookie sheets about 2 inches apart. Let them rise until puffy but not doubled (they should not be touching).

2. Brush with milk. Bake at 325°F until lightly golden brown, about 12 minutes.

For Doughnuts:

Roll out dough to a ½-inch thickness. Cut out with a doughnut cutter; then place on clean towels laid over cookie sheets or boards. Let rise until almost double; then fry in fat, heated to 350°–375°, about 4 inches deep. Keep fat at that temperature throughout the frying. Turn doughnuts once while frying, when they turn golden brown. Glaze, using the recipe below, or simply dust with sugar.

Doughnut Glaze

1 lb. confectioners' sugar
½ cup rich milk (or a bit more)
1 Tbsp. soft butter
1 tsp. vanilla

Heat together just until butter is melted and milk is warm. Glaze while doughnuts are hot.

CINNAMON FLOP

Makes two 9-inch pies.

Ingredients:

1 cup sugar
2 cups flour
2 tsp. baking powder
1 Tbsp. melted butter
1 cup milk
Brown sugar, cinnamon, and butter for top

Instructions:

1. Sift sugar, flour, and baking powder together. Add butter and milk and stir until well blended.

2. Divide mixture between two 9-inch pie or cake pans, well greased.

3. Sprinkle tops with flour, then brown sugar, then cinnamon. Push chunks of butter into the dough. This makes holes and later gets gooey as it bakes. Bake at 350°F for 30 minutes.

4. Cut into wedges and serve warm.

MASHED POTATO FILLING

Makes 10 servings.

Ingredients:

½ cup butter
½ cup celery, chopped
2 Tbsp. onion, chopped
4 cups soft bread cubes
½ cup boiling water
3 eggs, beaten
2 cups milk
1½ tsp. salt
2 cups mashed potatoes

Instructions:

1. Melt butter. Add celery and onion. Cook until tender. Pour over bread cubes and mix well.

2. Add boiling water to bread and mix well. Add remaining ingredients, mixing well after each addition. The finished product should be very moist.

3. Turn into 2 well-greased casserole dishes. Bake at 350°F for 45 minutes.

Recipe Notes: Almost a vegetable dish, this soft filling was likely invented by a cook who wanted to use up leftover mashed potatoes and stale bread. The final consistency of this traditional food is pudding-like.

GLAZED DOUGHNUTS

Makes about 5 dozen.

Ingredients:

1 cake yeast
1 cup warm water
1 cup scalded milk
½ cup sugar
1 tsp. salt
7 cups flour, sifted, divided
½ cup melted lard or shortening
2 eggs
1 tsp. vanilla

Instructions:

1. Dissolve yeast in warm water. Mix milk, sugar, and salt together. Cool to lukewarm. Add yeast mixture to milk.

2. Add 4 cups flour, one cup at a time, beating well after each addition.

3. Stir in lard, eggs, and vanilla. Add 3 more cups flour. Knead until smooth.

4. Let rise until doubled, about 2½ hours. Punch down, then roll to ½-inch thickness on floured surface.

5. Cut out doughnuts with doughnut cutter. Lay on clean towels over cookie sheets and let rise again until nearly double. Deep-fry in fat at 350°–370°F. Glaze while warm (see Doughnut Glaze recipe on page 17).

Recipe Notes: One tradition that continued among those women who mastered the earlier, less desirable flour and yeast, was doughnut-making. They mixed yeast doughs, then shaped them with a hole in the middle. An elderly Amish man remembers, "We'd have doughnuts at Christmastime or during butchering season when there was lard around. But I didn't know anything of *fastnachts* because we didn't keep Lent." In that, the Amish stand in contrast to their neighboring Pennsylvania Germans who are from a High Church tradition. Those folks, on Shrove Tuesday, bake *fastnachts* (a doughnut without a center hole, that is fried in lard) in a symbolic effort to rid their homes of leavening agents, and to feast before Lent.

A 40-year-old Amish woman fears that homemade doughnut-making may become a lost skill. "My mother made good doughnuts. She'd be asked to make the kind with holes in the middle for weddings. But now the young folks buy filled ones."

CREAM-FILLED DOUGHNUTS

Makes 2½ dozen.

Ingredients:
¾ cup lard or shortening
¾ cup sugar
1 cup hot water
2 packages dry yeast
1 cup warm water
2 eggs, beaten
1 tsp. salt
6 or more cups flour

Filling
4 cups confectioners' sugar
1½ cups shortening
2 egg whites
2 Tbsp. flour
2 tsp. vanilla
4 Tbsp. milk

Instructions:
1. In large bowl combine lard, sugar, and hot water. Add yeast to warm water and set aside to dissolve.

2. When mixture of lard, sugar, and hot water has cooled, add eggs, salt, yeast mixture, and flour.

3. Turn dough onto floured surface and knead until smooth and elastic. Cover and set in a warm place. Let rise until double. Roll dough about ½ inch thick and cut with drinking glass or doughnut cutter without the hole. Let rise again until double.

4. Fry doughnuts in deep fat until browned, turning once. Force filling into doughnut with a cookie press or cake decorator. If desired, sprinkle with sugar.

5. To make the filling, combine all filling ingredients and beat until smooth.

STICKY BUNS

Makes 2 dozen.

Ingredients:

1 package dry yeast
¼ cup warm water
¼ cup shortening
¼ cup sugar
1 cup milk, scalded, or 1 cup warm water
1 tsp. salt
1 egg, beaten
3¼–4 cups flour, divided
2 Tbsp. margarine or butter, softened

Instructions:

1. Dissolve yeast in warm water.

2. In large bowl, cream shortening and sugar. Pour hot milk or water over mixture. Cool to lukewarm. Add 1 cup flour and salt and beat well. Beat in yeast mixture and egg.

3. Gradually add remaining flour to form a soft dough, beating well.

4. Brush top of dough with softened margarine or butter. Cover and let rise in warm place until double (1½–2 hours).

5. Punch down and knead. Form rolls. Let rise again until doubled. Bake according to instructions below.

Recipe Notes: These breakfast favorites are also commonly known as Sweet Rolls, Cinnamon Rolls, or Pecan Stickies. The basic sweet roll dough adapts easily to varied glazes and fillings.
   These buns have made satisfying snacks before the late-afternoon milking. They also pack well into school lunch boxes.

For Cinnamon Rolls:

Divide dough in half. Roll each half into a rectangle, approximately 12-inch × 8-inch. Spread with butter and sprinkle with a mixture of ½ cup brown sugar and 1 tsp. cinnamon. Roll as a jelly roll. Cut into 1–1½-inch slices. Place rolls in greased pans about ¾ inch apart. Let rise and bake at 350°F for 30 minutes. Cool and spread with Doughnut Glaze (see page 17).

For Raisin Cinnamon Rolls:

Make rolls as above, but sprinkle with raisins before rolling up. Bake as above.

For Pecan Stickies:

1. Place ½ cup pecans in bottom of each of two greased 9½ × 5-inch × 3-inch pans. Make syrup by heating slowly: ½ cup brown sugar, ¼ cup butter, and 1 Tbsp. light corn syrup. Pour half of syrup over each pan of pecans. Prepare Cinnamon Rolls, using only ¼ cup brown sugar, and place rolls on top of pecans and syrup.

2. Let rise until double and bake at 375°F for about 25 minutes. Remove from oven and turn pan upside down unto a flat plate.

3. Syrup will run down through the rolls and pecans will be on top.

WAFFLES

Makes 10–12 waffles.

Ingredients:

4 eggs
2½ cups milk
¾ cup melted shortening
3½ cups flour
6 tsp. baking powder
1 tsp. salt

Instructions:

1. Combine all ingredients and beat for 1 minute.

2. Bake waffles in hot waffle iron.

Recipe Notes: Waffles are a rare treat; after all, how can one cook keep many hungry mouths happy with only one waffle iron? Some women tried, under less than ideal conditions!

"I remember Mother making waffles on the range," one graying grandmother smiled. "She would take the lid off and fit a round waffle iron down into the 'burner' opening above the flame on the range. It was a messy business, and hard to have the fire just right, so she didn't do it very often. And those were heavy waffles!"

Here is a lighter version that holds up under chicken gravy for a main meal or thickened fruit sauce for breakfast or a snack.

BREAD FILLING

Makes 6 servings.

Ingredients:

4 eggs
2 cups milk
2 quarts soft bread cubes
4 Tbsp. melted butter
1 tsp. onion, minced
1 tsp. salt
1 Tbsp. parsley, chopped (optional)
1 tsp. sage or poultry seasoning (optional)

Instructions:

1. Beat eggs. Add milk. Pour over bread cubes.

2. Combine butter and seasonings. Add to bread cubes and mix well.

3. Filling can be baked in a casserole dish at 350°F for 45 minutes or may be used as stuffing for fowl.

4. If baking in a casserole, cover tightly for the first 30 minutes, then remove cover to allow browning during the last 15 minutes of baking.

Recipe Notes: Bread crusts and stale bread are not problems for the resourceful Amish cook. Said one, "I just turn the crust to the inside when I'm making sandwiches and it doesn't make a difference to anyone!" But when bread passes its prime for eating as fresh slices, it is often dried to a crisp, then rolled into bread crumbs, or cubed and fashioned into Bread Filling.

A watchful cook can make this successfully on top of the stove. In fact, as one experienced Amish woman explained, "You don't even need gravy with it if you have it real moist." The dish is less likely to scorch, however, if it is baked in the oven.

Pies

The German settlers brought their love of pastries to Pennsylvania. What they learned from their English neighbors in the New World was how to fashion that fondness into pies. And pies have been on Amish menus ever since.

Considered nearly as essential as bread, pies were part of the weekly baking. A woman born in the 1920s remembers that her grandmother regularly baked 20 pies every Friday. "There were six children at home, plus a hired man. She always made shoofly and the rest were two-crust fruit pies. That's what they filled up on!"

Another woman of similar age explains, "I was the fifth oldest of 16 children, the second girl. My older sister got married when I was 14, so I had to take over the cooking. It took three pies for each meal. So when I baked, I'd make eight shoofly pies, eight pumpkin, and eight crumb pies."

In the Amish food tradition, pies have always defied confinement to one particular course or one meal or time of day. An 80-year-old grandmother says, "We ate our pies hot as a main meal." She also acknowledges that change has come. "We do that now with apple dumplings, but that's about all. We ate more starch then than we do now."

Pie is still commonly eaten as a breakfast food. Shoofly is often served, and with it, canned or fresh fruit and milk.

Pies are kept on tap as an accompaniment to soup, for dessert, for a pre-milking pick-me-up, for a bedtime snack. Pie is a tradition that has proven its adaptability through the years, even into this more health-conscious age. Most fruit pies can be made without a top crust, for example. Vegetable oil can be substituted for lard in the crust and the sugar content reduced in the filling. Too much tampering, however, can frustrate both the memory and experience of eating good pie! Here, then, are the old recipes.

PIECRUST

Makes six 9-inch pie shells or three 9-inch double-crust pies.

Ingredients:

4 cups flour
¾ tsp. salt
1 cup lard or vegetable shortening
1 egg, beaten
5 Tbsp. cold water
1 Tbsp. vinegar

Instructions:

1. Mix flour and salt. Cut in lard until mixture resembles small peas.

2. Combine remaining ingredients and stir into lard and flour. Let stand a few minutes.

3. Roll out dough on floured board.

Recipe Notes: The batter-stained, handwritten old cookbooks stashed in the kitchen drawers of most Amish cooks seldom contained instructions about how to make pie dough. If anything was there, it was a list of ingredients rather than a procedure. Those directions simply weren't needed. Mothers and grandmothers taught their daughters by showing them, and urging them to "feel" when the dough was right. But as one mother lamented, "A number of our girls work away from home now. When I learned to cook I was between 11 and 15. I tell our one daughter, who is a schoolteacher, that she must make at least one main meal a week so that she gets practice, and so she learns from me what she can before she's responsible for cooking for her own family."

APPLE PIE

Makes one 9-inch pie.

Ingredients:

6 cups apples, peeled and sliced
½–¾ cup sugar (depending upon the flavor of the apples)
2 Tbsp. flour
¾ tsp. cinnamon
2 Tbsp. lemon juice
1 (9-inch) unbaked pie shell and top crust

Instructions:

1. Toss apple slices gently with sugar, flour, cinnamon, and lemon juice. Spoon into unbaked pie shell.

2. Top with crust, folding its edge under the top of the bottom crust. Crimp to seal. Prick or cut slits in the top crust to allow steam to escape.

3. Bake at 425°F for 40–50 minutes, or until crust is golden brown.

Recipe Notes: "We had our own apples so we ate a lot of apple pie." It is a common theme when one probes the subject of the kinds of pies most often baked in Amish kitchens. Another woman in her mid-30s explains, "We ate a lot of apple pies; Mom made them with a top crust. For a full meal we would eat apple pie with potatoes alongside that were covered with brown butter. We'd eat it on a flat plate with a little bit of milk on the apple pie."

SOUR CHERRY PIE

Makes one 9-inch pie.

Ingredients:

3 cups sour cherries, drained
½ cup cherry juice
1 cup sugar
2 Tbsp. tapioca
⅛ tsp. salt
1 Tbsp. butter or margarine
1 (9-inch) unbaked pie shell plus top crust or lattice
  strips

Instructions:

1. Mix together cherries, juice, sugar, tapioca, and salt. Let stand for 15 minutes to allow thickening to begin.

2. Pour fruit mixture into pie shell. Dot with butter. Top with crust or lattice strips of pastry.

3. Bake at 425°F for 15 minutes, then reduce temperature to 350°F and bake an additional 35–40 minutes.

Recipe Notes: Sweetened sour cherries have a pungent tartness that makes them a favorite for pies. Cherry trees grow both wild and domestically in eastern Pennsylvania, so their natural presence has made their fruit an easily available dessert or snack. Since cherries retain their delectable qualities even when canned, cherry pies are prepared year-round.

RHUBARB PIE

Makes one 9-inch pie.

Ingredients:

Filling
3 cups diced rhubarb
1 (9-inch) unbaked pie shell
1¼ cups sugar
¼ tsp. salt
2 Tbsp. water
3 Tbsp. flour
1 Tbsp. lemon juice
2 eggs

Topping
3 Tbsp. flour
3 Tbsp. sugar
2 Tbsp. butter

Instructions:

1. Place rhubarb in unbaked pie shell.

2. Combine remaining ingredients and stir to form a smooth paste. Pour over rhubarb.

3. Mix together topping ingredients to form crumbs, then sprinkle over the top of the pie.

4. Bake at 425°F for 10 minutes, then at 325°F for 30 more minutes.

Recipe Notes: Sticking around an outbuilding on most Amish farms is a stand of rhubarb that puts in an appearance every spring.

Its sweetened tartness makes it a favorite in the Amish diet. Rhubarb is one more example of these people's pleasure in a zesty flavor that offsets another rich food, or whose own "bite" is only partly masked by the addition of sugar.

Rhubarb must be beloved in part because it is one of the first greens to flourish after a long winter without fresh food.

SCHNITZ PIE

Makes one 9-inch pie.

Ingredients:

3 cups dried apples
2¼ cups warm water
1 tsp. lemon extract
⅔ cup brown sugar
1 (9-inch) unbaked pie shell plus top crust

Instructions:

1. Soak apples in the warm water, then cook over low heat until soft.

2. Mash apples and add lemon and sugar.

3. Pour into unbaked pie shell. Cover with top crust. Seal edges.

4. Bake at 425°F for 15 minutes, then at 350°F for 30 minutes. Serve warm.

Recipe Notes: Since apple trees, which grow abundantly in eastern Pennsylvania, produced more apples than could be eaten fresh in most households, the German settlers dried much of their fruit. It was a home operation. The apples were peeled and cut into slices ("schnitz" means to cut into pieces), then laid on a roof or on racks above a heat source to dry.

Most apples dried in 24–48 hours, depending upon the thickness of the slices, the temperature of the heat source, and the temperature and humidity of the weather. Once dried, the sweet slices were stored in a dry container for use at any time of the year.

Today, schnitz pie is usually served at the lunch which follows the Sunday-morning church service.

Schnitz is now prepared commercially in Pennsylvania, so it is available to those without their own source of fresh apples.

HALF-MOON PIES

Makes 2–2½ dozen individual pies.

Ingredients:

2 quarts dried apples
3 cups water
1½ cups granulated sugar
1½ cups brown sugar
¾ tsp. cinnamon
1½ tsp. allspice
¾ tsp. salt
Piecrust (page 33) for 4 (9-inch) shells

Instructions:

1. Boil the dried apples in the water until the water is fully absorbed.

2. While they are cooking, prepare the piecrust dough. Then drain the apples. Blend in sugar and spices.

3. To form the individual pies, take a piece of dough about the size of an egg and shape it into a ball. Roll out into a circle until the dough is thin, yet able to hold the filling. Fold dough in half to form a crease through the center. Mark the top of one half with a pie crimper to shape the rounded edge.

4. Put ½ cup of the schnitz filling on the other half. Wet the outer edges of the dough. Fold the marked half over the half with the filling. Press edges together, cutting off ragged edges with the pie crimper.

5. Brush the tops with beaten egg, lift onto cookie sheets and bake at 425°F until golden brown.

Recipe Notes: A variation on schnitz pie developed in the Big Valley area of Pennsylvania, where an Amish settlement began in 1790. The Amish, who live west and south of Lewistown in the central part of the state, fashioned a schnitz pie that travels well—in the hand or in lunch boxes! Its name is descriptive of how the finished delicacy looks.

LEMON MERINGUE PIE

Makes one 9-inch pie.

Ingredients:

3 Tbsp. cornstarch
I cup sugar
Juice and zest of one lemon
3 egg yolks
I¼ cups boiling water
I (9-inch) baked pie shell

Meringue

3 egg whites
4 Tbsp. sugar

Instructions:

1. Add cornstarch and sugar to lemon juice and zest. Stir until smooth. Blend in egg yolks and then the boiling water.

2. Cook mixture in double boiler, stirring constantly until thickened.

3. Cool, then pour into baked pie shell. Top with meringue. Bake at 350°F until lightly golden (watch carefully!).

4. Beat whites stiffly. Fold in sugar, one tablespoon at a time. Pile onto lemon pie.

LEMON SPONGE PIE

Makes one 9-inch pie.

Ingredients:

1 cup sugar
2 Tbsp. butter
3 eggs, separated
3 Tbsp. flour
½ tsp. salt
Juice and zest of 1 lemon
1½ cups hot water or milk
1 (9-inch) unbaked pie shell

Instructions:

1. Cream sugar and butter. Add egg yolks and beat well. Add flour, salt, and lemon juice and zest. Add water or milk. Fold in stiffly beaten egg whites.

2. Pour into unbaked pie shell. Bake at 325°F for 45–50 minutes.

Recipe Notes: Lemon pies were a treat. Citrus fruit does not grow in eastern Pennsylvania. But the area's proximity to the canals that webbed their way as far west as Ohio and provided waterways to the Atlantic coastal cities made it possible to get lemons and oranges. Some farmers sold their hay in Philadelphia and could bring home the treats available there.

In many homes, lemon pies were made primarily when company was coming.

SHOOFLY PIE

Makes one 9-inch pie.

Crumbs

I cup flour
⅔ cup light brown sugar
I Tbsp. shortening

Bottom Part

I egg, slightly beaten
I cup molasses
I cup boiling water
I tsp. baking soda
I (9-inch) unbaked pie shell

Instructions:

1. Mix flour and sugar. Cut in shortening. Take out ½ cup crumbs and set aside.

2. To larger portion of crumb mixture, add egg and molasses. Blend in ¾ cup boiling water. Dissolve baking soda in remaining ¼ cup water and add last.

3. Pour into unbaked pie shell. Sprinkle reserved crumbs on top. Bake at 425°F for 15 minutes. Reduce heat to 350°F and bake for 40–45 minutes longer.

Recipe Notes: This cakey pie, with a name that has produced a myriad of reasons for its existence, may have its roots in the early bake ovens of Pennsylvania. Dense cakes with heavy dough were put into the bake ovens following the weekly bread-baking, which required the hottest fires. This hybrid cake within a pie shell weathered the bake oven well. It was with the advent of the kitchen range and its more easily controlled temperatures that lighter pies with custards, creams, and more delicate fruit became common.

MONTGOMERY PIE

Makes three 9-inch pies.

Bottom

Juice and zest of one lemon
1 cup molasses
2 cups water
1 cup sugar
3 Tbsp. flour
1 egg
3 (9-inch) unbaked pie shells

Top

½ cup butter
2 cups sugar
2 eggs
2½ cups flour
2½ tsp. baking powder
1 cup milk

Instructions:

1. Blend first six ingredients until smooth. Pour into 3 pie shells.

2. To make the top part, cream butter and sugar. Add eggs and beat thoroughly. Combine flour and baking powder. Add milk alternately with dry ingredients.

3. Divide batter and pour over the syrup in the pie shells.

4. Bake at 450°F for 15 minutes; reduce heat to 350°F and continue baking for another 45 minutes.

Recipe Notes: Pies with cakey tops and a variety of syrupy flavored bottoms are remembered especially by the older members of the Amish community. This cake in a pie shell is related to the more common shoofly pie, although its lemon-flavored bottom is reminiscent of lemon sponge pie.

VANILLA PIE

Makes one 9-inch pie.

Ingredients:

¼ cup granulated sugar

¼ cup brown sugar

½ cup molasses or light corn syrup

I cup water

I egg, well beaten

I Tbsp. flour

I tsp. vanilla

I (9-inch) unbaked pie shell

Crumbs

¼ cup lard, butter, margarine, or vegetable shortening

I cup flour

½ tsp. baking powder

½ tsp. baking soda

½ cup brown sugar

Instructions:

1. Combine all the ingredients, except the vanilla, in a saucepan. Bring to a boil and continue boiling until it becomes a thick syrup.

2. Allow to cool and stir in vanilla. Pour into unbaked shell.

3. To make the crumbs, melt lard and stir in dry ingredients. Crumble over syrup. Bake at 375°F for 50–60 minutes.

Recipe Notes: Vanilla pie is a close cousin to shoofly pie, distinguished from it mostly by the presence of vanilla in the syrupy bottom part.

PUMPKIN PIE

Makes one 9-inch pie.

Ingredients:

1½ cups mashed pumpkin or butternut squash

1 egg

½ cup milk, heated

½ cup cream, heated

1 Tbsp. flour

1 Tbsp. molasses or King Syrup

¾ cup sugar

1 tsp. cinnamon

Dash of nutmeg

1 Tbsp. brown butter

Pinch of salt

1 (9-inch) unbaked pie shell

Instructions:

1. Combine all ingredients. Pour into unbaked pie shell. Sprinkle additional cinnamon and nutmeg over top of pie.

2. Bake at 450°F for 15 minutes; then at 350°F for 45 minutes.

Recipe Notes: Gooseneck pumpkins grow in southeastern Pennsylvania. With some experimentation, and likely through association with their English neighbors, the German settlers discovered the pleasure of pumpkin, in combination with molasses, eggs, spices, and cream. It became a regularly prepared pie in Amish homes, with little or no connection to Thanksgiving or Christmas.

CUSTARD PIE

Makes one 9-inch pie.

Ingredients:

⅓ cup sugar

2 tsp. flour

½ tsp. salt

3 eggs

3 cups milk, divided

1 (9-inch) unbaked pie shell

¼ tsp. nutmeg

Instructions:

1. Combine sugar, flour, salt, and eggs and mix until smooth.

2. Heat milk to boiling point. Add 1 cup hot milk to egg mixture. Pour that into the remaining hot milk.

3. Pour into unbaked pie shell. Sprinkle nutmeg over the top. Bake at 350°F for 40–45 minutes.

Recipe Notes: Most Amish families' egg supplies have come from their own flocks of chickens. When there were plenty of eggs, the cook had a repertoire of dishes to make so that no eggs went to waste (fried or scrambled for breakfast or lunch, in sandwiches or on top of stewed crackers, mixed into noodles or angel food cake, and more). Custard pies were a welcome variation to the usual weekly fare.

PEACH PIE

Makes one 9-inch pie.

Ingredients:
4 cups peaches, peeled and sliced
½ cup sugar
¼ tsp. salt
2½ Tbsp. tapioca
1 (9-inch) unbaked pie shell

Instructions:
1. Mix together gently peaches, sugar, salt, and tapioca together gently. Let blend for 5 minutes before spooning into pie shell. Top with crumbs.
2. Bake at 425°F for 45–50 minutes.

Recipe Notes: From mid-July through the end of August, peaches are in full supply in eastern Pennsylvania. Family orchards produce some; fruit farms raise them in abundance.
   The Amish woman cans dozens of jars of peaches, but saves many for eating fresh—simply cut in slices or over shortcake or in pies.

Crumbs
2½ Tbsp. butter or margarine, melted
¼ cup flour
½ tsp. cinnamon
⅓ cup brown sugar

Instructions:
Mix together until crumbly and sift over pie.

PEAR PIE

Makes one 9-inch pie.

Ingredients:

¼ cup flour

¾ cup sugar

1 cup cream

1 Tbsp. lemon juice

5 fresh pears, peeled and diced, or canned pears in
light syrup

1 (9-inch) unbaked pie shell

1 Tbsp. sugar

¼ tsp. cinnamon

Instructions:

1. Sift together flour and sugar. Stir in cream and lemon juice. Mix until smooth. Add pears. Pour into an unbaked pie shell. Sprinkle top with sugar and cinnamon.

2. Bake at 400°F for 45–50 minutes. Cool until set.

Recipe Notes: Many farmsteads had a wild Seckel pear tree growing somewhere on the acreage. It was the domesticated pear trees in the family orchard or on local fruit farms, however, that provided the fruit for the seasonal pear pies. Canned pears could also be used to bring occasional variety to the family's pie diet.

GROUND-CHERRY PIE

Makes one 9-inch pie.

Ingredients:

3½ cups ground-cherries

3 cups water, divided

⅓ cup cornstarch

1¼ cups sugar

¼ tsp. salt

2 Tbsp. lemon juice

2 tsp. unflavored gelatin

1 (9-inch) unbaked pie shell and top crust

Instructions:

1. Cook ground-cherries in 1½ cups water until mixture comes to a boil.

2. Meanwhile, mix together cornstarch, sugar, salt, and ¾ cup water until smooth. Stir into boiling cherries until fruit thickens.

3. Remove from heat and stir in lemon juice.

4. Soak gelatin in ½ cup water. Add to fruit mixture, stirring well.

5. Spoon into unbaked pie shell and add top crust. Bake at 400°F for 15 minutes; reduce heat to 375°F and bake 30 minutes longer.

Recipe Notes: Ground-cherries grow wild in the Pennsylvania countryside. Stewards of the earth's bounty, the Amish picked them for food, discovering them to be a tasty filling for pies.

GRAPE PIE

Makes one 9-inch pie.

Ingredients:

3 cups Concord grapes
½–¾ cup sugar
3 Tbsp. flour
1 Tbsp. lemon juice
1 Tbsp. butter
1 (9-inch) unbaked pie shell and top crust

Instructions:

1. Stem grapes, wash, drain, and squeeze from skins. Set skins aside. Simmer remaining pulp for 5 minutes.

2. Remove from heat and immediately put through food press (this will separate the seeds from the usable pulp).

3. Stir pulp and skins together. Blend in sugar and flour. Add lemon juice and butter.

4. Spoon into pie shell. Cover with top crust.

5. Bake at 425°F for 10 minutes; reduce temperature to 350°F and bake for an additional 30 minutes.

Recipe Notes: Concord grape arbors shade many Amish porches. Their summer fruit yields gallons of juice, batches of jam, and an occasional pie. The skins and seeds are obstacles to overcome, but the tangy flavor makes the effort worthwhile.

Variation:

Combine 1 cup flour, ½ cup sugar, and ¼ cup melted butter and mix together until crumbly. Sprinkle over pie in place of the top crust.

RAISIN PIE

Makes one 9-inch pie.

Ingredients:

2 cups raisins
2 cups cold water, divided
1½ cups sugar, divided
4 Tbsp. flour
2 eggs, separated
¼ tsp. salt
4 Tbsp. melted butter
1 Tbsp. vinegar or lemon juice
1 (9-inch) baked pie shell

Instructions:

1. In saucepan combine raisins, 1½ cups cold water, and 1 cup sugar and bring to a boil. Combine the remaining ½ cup water and ½ cup sugar, plus flour, egg yolks, and salt; add to raisin mixture.

2. Cook until thickened, stirring constantly. Remove from heat and add butter and vinegar or lemon juice.

3. Pour mixture into baked pie shell. Cover with whipped cream or meringue.

Recipe Notes: Raisin pie was not on the weekly menu. "We had to buy the raisins. It just wasn't as common as cherry because we grew our own cherries."

In contrast to some groups of Germanic heritage, the Lancaster Amish of this century do not—and have no memory of—serving raisin pie at their funerals. "We often have stewed prunes, but raisin pies are not a funeral tradition," said a minister's wife, whose explanation was corroborated by several others of varying ages.

The most traditional pie is one in which the raisins are stewed in water and that juice is thickened, rather than a cream pie to which milk is added.

Meringue Instructions:

Beat 2 egg whites till stiff peaks form. Gradually add 2 Tbsp. sugar while beating. Pile on top of pie and bake at 350°F till golden brown, about 10 minutes.

HUCKLEBERRY PIE

Makes one 9-inch pie.

Ingredients:

2¾ cups huckleberries

1 (9-inch) unbaked pie shell and top crust

½ cup berry juice or 3 Tbsp. lemon juice with water added to make ½ cup liquid

½ cup sugar

2 Tbsp. flour

Instructions:

1. Stem and wash huckleberries. Spoon into pie shell.

2. Mix juice, sugar, and flour together and pour over berries. Cover with top crust, folding under top edge of bottom crust.

3. Bake at 425°F for 10 minutes. Reduce temperature to 350°F and bake for 30 minutes more.

Recipe Notes: "Huckle picking was an outing," recalls an Amish grandfather. "We'd get up early, pack our lunches, and go down to the Welsh Mountain. There had been a forest fire years before, and huckleberry bushes grew up where the trees once stood.

"We would pick while the day was still cool. When it got hot we ate our lunches, picked some more, then took the berries home to can them. Often several of us families would go together."

Huckleberries are a kind of wild blueberry. Blueberries may be used in this recipe; the sugar may be adjusted depending upon the tartness of the berries.

MINCEMEAT PIE

Makes one 9-inch pie.

Ingredients:

Beef bone yielding 2 cups cooked meat, cut in small
  pieces
1½ cups raisins
3 cups apples, peeled and chopped fine
½ cup brown sugar
⅓ cup fresh orange sections, cut up in small pieces
¼ cup fresh lemon sections, cut up in small pieces
¼ tsp. salt
1 tsp. cinnamon
½ tsp. cloves
⅓ cup cider
1 (9-inch) unbaked pie shell and top crust

Instructions:

1. Simmer beef bone until meat is tender. Cut in fine pieces. Combine beef with remaining ingredients and simmer for 10–15 minutes (add beef broth if needed to keep mixture from getting dry).

2. Pour into unbaked pie shell. Cover with top crust; seal edges thoroughly.

3. Bake at 425°F for 15 minutes, then reduce temperature to 375°F and bake for another 35 minutes.

Recipe Notes: Mincemeat pie likely had its beginnings during medieval times when spiced meat dishes were the order of the day and served as the main meal rather than dessert.

It is probable that the Pennsylvania Germans learned this recipe from their English neighbors. Mincemeat pie fits well the needs of German farmers. It is a hearty meal—the meat was a by-product of home-butchering, and the additional fruits could be varied according to the dried or canned supply that was in the attic or cellar.

One grandmother remembers, "We'd eat it at butchering time. But Mom canned the mincemeat so we could have it anytime. Now I think I can't make it because we don't butcher. You see, Mom would cook the beef bones and then pick off the last bits of meat. Using the bones gave the meat and broth a full flavor you don't get otherwise, and it used up every corner of the meat!"

GREEN TOMATO PIE

Makes one 9-inch pie.

Ingredients:

2 Tbsp. flour
1 (9-inch) unbaked pie shell and top crust
4 cups green tomatoes, sliced thin (leave parings on)
1 cup granulated sugar
½ cup brown sugar
3 Tbsp. lemon juice
1 tsp. cinnamon
½ tsp. cloves
1 Tbsp. butter or margarine

Instructions:

1. Sprinkle flour over bottom of pie shell. Layer slices of tomatoes into pie plate.

2. Mix sugars, lemon juice, and spices together. Pour over tomatoes. Dot with butter.

3. Cover with top crust. Bake at 425°F for 15 minutes, then reduce temperature to 375°F and bake for an additional 30 minutes.

Recipe Notes: Amish cooks can only speculate about the origin of green tomato pie: "In the fall people wanted to use up their excess tomatoes, so they made this pie." Suggests another, "Maybe it was to help out in an emergency—'What shall we make for supper?!'" "Maybe green tomato pie developed to supplement the apple supply, which at that season of the year was nearly depleted." Another remembers, "Mother used to make it because she really liked it and so did my father. I think she made it as a special treat for him. I didn't care for it that much, but we didn't have to eat dessert! It did provide a little variety in the pies we ate."

It has been noted that the seasonings that accompany the green tomatoes are much the same as those that flavor mincemeat pie, another fall dish.

WALNUT PIE

Makes two 9-inch pies.

Ingredients:

1 cup warm water

¾ cup molasses

2 eggs, well beaten

1 cup sweet milk

4 Tbsp. flour

½ cup walnuts, chopped

2 (9-inch) baked pie crusts

Instructions:

1. Bring water and molasses to a boil. Meanwhile, stir together beaten eggs, milk, and flour until smooth. Mix into water and molasses and let boil until thick.

2. Remove from heat and add walnuts. When cool, pour into baked crusts.

Recipe Notes: Black walnut trees used to grow wild along the fencerows bordering many Amish farms. The wood from these trees is now in such high demand that comparatively few of them remain. Despite the fact that the nuts were difficult to shell and stained the hands of the sheller with a black, acidic liquid, the nuts were freely harvested and mixed into cakes and pies.

Their flavor is strong and penetrating, so only a relative few are needed to enliven the taste of the dessert of which they are a part. This is a rich dish for special times.

PECAN PIE

Makes one 8-inch pie.

Ingredients:

2 Tbsp. butter or margarine
¼ cup sugar
2 eggs
¾ cup molasses
1 Tbsp. flour
1 tsp. vanilla
Pinch of salt
¾ cup water
½ cup pecans
1 (8-inch) unbaked pie shell

Instructions:

1. Cream butter, sugar, and eggs. Add molasses, flour, vanilla, and salt. Stir in water and pecans.

2. Pour into unbaked pie shell. Bake at 450°F for 10 minutes, then reduce temperature to 350°F for an additional 25–30 minutes.

Recipe Notes: Pecans were a rare treat, but not unknown to the Amish because of eastern Pennsylvania's access to goods that passed through Philadelphia and Baltimore. Pecan pie is another demonstration of the preference for a salty-sweet combination of flavors found throughout the Amish diet (sweet-and-sour bacon salad dressing, ham and green beans with sweet-and-sour coleslaw, and syrup over mush and scrapple are other examples).

Cakes & Cookies

Cakes and cookies, while never as passionately sought after as pies, were still a fixture in the Amish pantry. They likely entered the diet later than pies since they were more dependent upon refined flour and finely tuned temperatures than were available in the early bake ovens.

Perhaps it was because of those "dry" beginnings that cakes and cookies are commonly—and openly—"dunked" when served. The practice is neither regarded as poor manners nor as an insult to the cook. "Dunking is the way to eat cookies and cakes," explains an elderly woman, smiling. Individual preferences vary, of course, "We dunk cookies in milk or hot tea," offers a mother of five children, all under the age of nine. "At harvesttime," remembers an older man, "we'd get a pretty good snack at dark and then I'd dunk that in root beer." "I just prefer to take a bite and then a sip. I don't like all those crumbs floating in my coffee and water," says a middle-aged woman.

Basic to many cake batters are eggs and sweet or sour milk—ingredients in good supply on a farm. Although the Amish settlers cannot claim credit for developing these recipes, the cakes and cookies that became their favorites have been particularly well suited to their lives. Most are substantial; most require few steps in their procedures and so can be whipped up in large quantities, either for sizable families or for sale at market stands.

These cakes and cookies make hearty breakfasts, they top off any meal, they travel well in school lunches, and they brighten a mid-afternoon snack in the fields.

CHOCOLATE CAKE

Makes I long or I layer cake.

Ingredients:

I cup brown sugar
I cup granulated sugar
I cup lard or vegetable shortening
2 eggs, unbeaten
I cup buttermilk
2¾ cups flour
½ cup cocoa powder
½ cup boiling water
I tsp. baking soda

Instructions:

1. Cream sugars and lard. Mix in eggs, buttermilk, flour, and cocoa until well blended.

2. Dissolve baking soda in boiling water, then stir into batter.

3. Pour into greased and floured round layer cake pans or into a long pan, 9-inch × 13-inch. Bake at 350°F for 25–35 minutes. Test for doneness before removing from oven.

Recipe Notes: "The cake we ate most at home was chocolate," reports an Amish woman with slightly graying hair. "It was usually baked in a long pan, and dusted with confectioners' sugar rather than iced." Her memory is echoed by many others, no matter their ages.

HOT MILK SPONGE CAKE

Makes one 9-inch × 13-inch or tube pan cake.

Ingredients:

4 eggs

2 cups granulated sugar

2 tsp. flavoring (optional)

2 Tbsp. butter or margarine, melted

1 cup hot milk

2 cups flour

½ tsp. salt

2 tsp. baking powder

Instructions:

1. Beat eggs and sugar together until light. Mix together flavoring, butter or margarine, and hot milk. Stir into eggs and sugar and blend thoroughly.

2. Sift together dry ingredients. Fold lightly into batter until smooth.

3. Bake in either a greased and floured 9-inch × 13-inch cake pan at 350°F for 25–30 minutes or in a tube pan (do not grease or flour) at 350°F for 45 minutes.

Recipe Notes: A woman born at the turn of the twentieth century once recalled, "We baked a lot of sponge cakes." The favored cake came from Germany and continued as a specialty here. Eggs were usually plentiful and could be put to good use in this batter. The cake was also adaptable—the cook could add her choice of flavoring before baking, or she could leave it out and serve the cake with fresh strawberries (or whatever fruit was easily at hand).

ICE WATER WHITE CAKE

Makes 1 layer cake.

Ingredients:

½ cup butter or margarine
2 cups granulated sugar
3½ cups cake flour
½ tsp. salt
3 tsp. baking powder
1½ cups ice water
¼ tsp. almond flavoring (optional)
4 eggs whites, stiffly beaten

Instructions:

1. Cream butter. Gradually add sugar, beating until fluffy.

2. Sift dry ingredients together. Add alternately with ice water and flavoring, if desired, to creamed butter.

3. Fold in stiffly beaten egg whites.

4. Bake in 2 greased cake layer pans at 350°F for 30 minutes. Remove from pans, cool, and frost as desired.

ANGEL FOOD CAKE

Makes 1 large cake.

Ingredients:

1½ cups cake flour
2¼ cups granulated sugar
2½ cups egg whites (18 eggs)
3 Tbsp. water
¼ tsp. salt
1½ tsp. cream of tartar
1½ tsp. vanilla

Instructions:

1. Sift the flour. Add ¾ cup sugar and sift with flour three times. Set aside.

2. Beat the egg whites with a rotary beater (not an electric mixer) until foamy. Add salt and cream of tartar. Continue beating until the whites hold peaks. Slowly add the rest of the sugar to the beaten egg whites, folding it in gently. Add the vanilla.

3. Sift the flour and sugar mixture, a tablespoon at a time, over the beaten egg whites. Fold in lightly.

4. Pour well blended mixture into a 12-inch × 14-inch ungreased tube pan. Bake at 350°F for one hour. When finished, turn the cake upside down to cool. Frost with a butter icing if desired.

Recipe Notes: Angel food cakes are not an extravagance on a farm where eggs are plentiful. In fact, the cake was often baked on the same day as noodles were made. Noodles required the yolks; angel food cakes the egg whites.

An experienced cook, who learned to bake the delicacy as a 14-year-old, says that the cake turns out best if the eggs are beaten by hand rather than with an electric mixer. "If you beat the eggs too fast, the foam goes down. I always used a wire whisk at home."

This light, mildly flavored cake is enhanced when crushed strawberries are served over it.

CHOCOLATE ANGEL FOOD CAKE

Makes 1 large cake.

Ingredients:

¾ cup cake flour

¼ cup cocoa

¼ tsp. salt

1 tsp. cream of tartar

2 cups egg whites (14 to 16 whites)

1 tsp. vanilla

1½ cups granulated sugar

Instructions:

1. Sift flour, cocoa, and salt together.

2. Blend the cream of tartar into the egg whites and beat them until they peak softly. Gently fold in the vanilla, then fold in the sugar, a tablespoon at a time.

3. Pour into an ungreased tube pan and bake at 350°F for 40–45 minutes. When cake is finished, invert to cool.

Recipe Notes: Recalls a woman in her mid-50s, "We always liked chocolate angel food cake better than white because it has more flavor." She was the family's angel-food-cake baker on noodle-making days.

OLD-FASHIONED CRUMB CAKE

Makes 1 long cake.

Ingredients:

3 cups flour

2 cups brown sugar

½ cup butter or margarine

1 egg, beaten

1 cup buttermilk

1 tsp. baking soda

1 tsp. cream of tartar

Instructions:

1. Mix flour and brown sugar together. Cut in butter or margarine until mixture is crumbly. Take out 1 cup crumbs for topping.

2. Add to remaining crumbs the egg, buttermilk, baking soda, and cream of tartar. Mix well after each addition.

3. Pour into a greased 9-inch × 13-inch baking pan. Sprinkle reserved cup of crumbs over top. Bake at 375°F for 25–35 minutes.

Recipe Notes: A moist coffee cake that is enhanced when eaten with applesauce, peaches, or pears. It needs no icing.

SHOOFLY CAKE

Makes 1 long cake.

Ingredients:

4 cups flour (use 2 cups whole wheat flour and
  2 cups white flour, if desired)

2 cups brown sugar

1 cup butter or margarine

2 cups boiling water

1 cup molasses

2 tsp. baking soda

Instructions:

1. Work the flour, sugar, and butter into fine crumbs with your fingers or a pastry mixer. Set aside 1½ cups crumbs for topping.

2. Mix water, molasses, and baking soda together. Then add to the remaining crumbs. Mix until batter is very thin yet still lumpy.

3. Pour into greased and floured 9-inch × 13-inch cake pan. Sprinkle with reserved crumbs. Bake at 350°F for 35 minutes.

Recipe Notes: This close kin to shoofly pie has no crust; consequently, it can be put together more quickly. The crumb topping and gooey bottom make an icing unnecessary. It is best served when slightly warm, fresh from the oven.

SPICE CAKE

Makes 1 layer cake or 1 long cake.

Ingredients:

2 cups brown sugar

½ cup butter

2 eggs

1 cup sour milk

2½ cups sifted flour

1½ tsp. baking power

1 tsp. cinnamon

1 tsp. nutmeg

1 tsp. baking soda

1 tsp. vanilla

Instructions:

1. Cream sugar and butter together until fluffy. Add eggs and beat until light.

2. Sift together all dry ingredients, then add them alternately with the milk to the creamed mixture, beating well after each addition. Mix in the vanilla.

3. Pour into greased layer pans or a 9-inch × 13-inch cake pan. Bake at 350°F for 35–40 minutes.

Recipe Notes: This soft, gingerbread-like cake can vary slightly in its subtle flavoring by interchanging the spices used, depending upon one's own and family's preferences.

Variations:

- Use cloves instead of nutmeg.

- Add 1 tsp. allspice to dry ingredients.

- Add 1 tsp. cloves to dry ingredients.

1-2-3-4 POUND CAKE

Makes 1 large loaf cake.

Ingredients:

1 cup butter

2 cups sugar

4 eggs

3 cups cake flour (or use 2½ cups
cake flour and ½ cup cocoa)

½ tsp. salt

3 tsp. baking powder

1 cup sour cream

1 tsp. vanilla

Instructions:

1. Cream butter, then add sugar gradually and beat until fluffy.

2. Add eggs, one by one, beating well after each addition.

3. Sift dry ingredients together. Mix sour cream and vanilla. Add dry ingredients and sour cream mixture alternately to butter-sugar-egg batter, beating well continuously.

4. Bake in a large, greased bread pan at 350°F for 1 hour.

Recipe Notes: "We often baked this 1-2-3-4 cake. For a variation sometimes we would fill the last cup of flour with cocoa," remembers an 80-year-old woman who raised—and cooked for—a large family.

OATMEAL CAKE

Makes one 9-inch × 13-inch cake

Ingredients:

1 cup rolled oats
1¼ cups boiling water
½ cup butter or margarine
1 cup granulated sugar
1 cup brown sugar
2 eggs
1 tsp. baking soda
½ tsp. salt
1 tsp. cinnamon
1⅔ cup flour
1 tsp. vanilla

Topping

6 Tbsp. butter or margarine, melted
¼ cup milk or cream
1 cup brown sugar
½ cup nuts, chopped

Instructions:

1. Mix oats and boiling water together; set aside for 20 minutes.

2. Cream butter or margarine and sugars together thoroughly. Add eggs, one at a time, beating well after each one. Blend in oatmeal mixture.

3. Sift together remaining dry ingredients. Fold into batter. Stir in vanilla.

4. Pour into greased and floured 9-inch × 13-inch baking pan. Bake at 350°F for 30–35 minutes.

5. After baking, but before the cake cools, mix together all topping ingredients, spread mixture over cake, and broil about 2 minutes or until it browns. Watch carefully since it burns easily!

HICKORY NUT CAKE

Makes 1 layer cake.

Ingredients:

½ cup butter or margarine, softened

1¾ cups granulated sugar

3 cups flour

3 tsp. baking powder

1 cup milk

1½ tsp. vanilla

1 cup hickory nuts

5 egg whites, beaten until stiff

Instructions:

1. Cream butter or margarine and sugar together. Mix together flour and baking powder. Add dry ingredients alternately with milk to creamed butter and sugar.

2. Blend in vanilla. Stir in nuts. Fold in egg whites.

3. Bake in 2 greased and floured cake pans at 350°F for 30 minutes.

Recipe Notes: These nuts from the trees that grow wild on the fencerows flavor cakes as well as pies. The beaten egg whites (eggs were generally in good supply on the farm) make this an airy dessert.

MOLASSES CAKE

Makes one 8-inch square cake.

Ingredients:

¾ cup molasses

1 egg

½ cup sour milk or buttermilk

1½ cups flour

1 tsp. baking soda

¼ cup boiling water

Instructions:

1. Combine molasses, egg, and milk thoroughly. Stir in flour.

2. Dissolve baking soda in boiling water, then add to batter.

3. Bake in a greased and floured 8-inch square cake pan at 375°F for 30–45 minutes.

Recipe Notes: Molasses was sometimes more available than sugar. A favorite topping for mush, it was a common ingredient in the pantry or cellar.

RHUBARB CAKE

Makes 1 long cake.

Ingredients:

½ cup butter or margarine
1 cup granulated sugar
1 egg
1 tsp. vanilla
2 cups plus 2 Tbsp. flour
1 tsp. cinnamon
1 tsp. baking soda
½ tsp. salt
1 cup buttermilk or sour milk
2 cups rhubarb, finely cut
½ cup chopped nuts (optional)
½ cup grated coconut (optional)
½ cup raisins (optional)

Instructions:

1. Cream together butter or margarine and sugar. Blend in egg and vanilla.

2. Mix together flour, cinnamon, baking soda, and salt. Add alternately with milk to creamed mixture.

3. Stir in rhubarb and any or all of the optional ingredients, mixing thoroughly.

4. Pour into a greased 9-inch × 13-inch baking pan. Bake at 350°F for 45 minutes.

Recipe Notes: Rhubarb brings moistness and piquancy to coffee cake. This satisfies those family members and guests who prefer a hint of rhubarb rather than the full flavor of a rhubarb pie.

BUTTER CREAM ICING

———◆•⌘•◆———

Icing for 1 long cake.

Ingredients:
3 Tbsp. butter or margarine
1½ cups confectioners' sugar
1 Tbsp. cream or milk
½ tsp. vanilla

Instructions:

1. Beat butter until smooth. Cream in (by hand or electric mixer) the sugar.

2. When smooth, add cream or milk and vanilla, beating until creamy.

Recipe Notes: Icings were traditionally prepared for special company or were simple additions to those cakes that seemed to need something extra. "We often ate our cakes without icing, just dusted with confectioners' sugar," commented a woman in her early 40s. A woman 10 years older explains her method, "Just beat margarine or butter with confectioners' sugar and a little milk and vanilla. That's what we used to do and what I still do."

That traditional unwritten recipe has been transcribed for those who don't cook "by feel."

SEVEN-MINUTE ICING

Icing for a layer cake.

Ingredients:

2 egg whites, unbeaten
1½ cups granulated sugar
5 Tbsp. cold water
1 tsp. light corn syrup
1 tsp. vanilla

Instructions:

1. Mix together egg whites, sugar, water, and corn syrup in top section of double boiler. Place over rapidly boiling water and beat continuously with a rotary beater for 7 minutes. Remove from heat.

2. Stir in vanilla and continue beating until icing is able to be spread.

Recipe Notes: A commonly used recipe that measures the beating time—by hand—required for the icing to reach proper consistency.

CARAMEL ICING

Makes enough for one 8-inch single-layer cake.

Ingredients:

½ cup butter or margarine

1 cup brown sugar

¼ cup milk

1¾–2 cups sifted confectioners' sugar

Instructions:

1. Melt butter in saucepan. Add brown sugar and cook over low heat for 2 minutes, stirring constantly.

2. Add milk and continue stirring until mixture comes to a boil.

3. Remove from heat and cool. Add confectioners' sugar until frosting reaches desired consistency.

Recipe Notes: "My mother liked a caramel icing made with brown sugar. She didn't really have a recipe." This grandmother's account is typical. Here is a written approximation of what she enjoyed on chocolate cake.

SOUR CREAM SUGAR COOKIES

Makes about 3 dozen

Ingredients:

1½ cups sugar

1 cup margarine

2 eggs

1 cup sour cream or buttermilk

3¾ cups flour

2 tsp. baking powder

1 tsp. soda

1 tsp. vanilla

Instructions:

1. Cream sugar and margarine. Add eggs and beat well.

2. Add sour cream, dry ingredients, and vanilla and mix thoroughly.

3. Drop by teaspoonsful onto greased cookie sheet. Bake at 375°F for 8–10 minutes.

Variations:

- Use 1 tsp. lemon extract in place of vanilla.

- Place a raisin in the center and sprinkle the top of each cookie with sugar before baking.

Recipe Notes: Sugar cookies' plain looks belie the emotion that sugar-cookie connoisseurs carry about them.

"Our favorites were sugar cookies with a little confectioners' sugar sprinkled on top."

"We ate lots of sugar cookies, sometimes with a little lemon in the batter."

"We made our batter with sour cream, rolled out the dough and put a raisin on top of each."

"I can't make them like my mother, who used buttermilk!"

"Drop sugar cookies are much more common than rolled-out ones."

"I make drop sugar cookies but my mother made rolled ones. Hers were spongy soft. When they're rolled and cut out, they rise to the same height all over."

Here is the first of five batters—4 family-size batters and one crowd-size to make with visitors.

BROWN SUGAR COOKIES

Makes 10–11 dozen cookies.

Ingredients:

3 cups brown sugar
1 cup lard, butter, or margarine, softened
2 eggs
2 tsp. baking soda
2 cups sour milk
2 tsp. baking powder
Pinch of salt
5 cups flour, sifted

Instructions:

1. Cream together the brown sugar, lard, and eggs.

2. Stir baking soda into sour milk.

3. Sift baking powder, salt, and flour together. Add milk and dry ingredients alternately to creamed mixture.

4. Drop by teaspoonful onto greased cookie sheets. Bake at 350°F for 7–8 minutes.

DROP SUGAR COOKIES

Makes 10–11 dozen cookies.

Ingredients:

1 cup shortening, softened
2 cups granulated sugar
2 eggs
2 tsp. baking soda
4 tsp. baking powder
¼ tsp. salt
1 tsp. vanilla
1 cup milk
5 cups flour

Instructions:

1. Cream together shortening, sugar, and eggs. Mix in baking soda, baking powder, salt, and vanilla.

2. Add milk and flour alternately to creamed mixture.

3. Drop by teaspoonful onto greased cookie sheets.

4. Bake at 350°F for 10–12 minutes.

Icing

6 Tbsp. butter (at room temperature)
2 tsp. vanilla
Dash of salt
1 pound confectioners' sugar, sifted
4–5 Tbsp. milk

Instructions:

Mix all ingredients together for 1 minute. Spread on cooled cookies, or first divide into several parts and add different food colors to each part, to give variety.

ROLLED SOUR CREAM SUGAR COOKIES

Makes about 13–15 dozen cookies.

Ingredients:

3 cups granulated sugar

1 cup lard, butter, or margarine

5 eggs

2 tsp. baking soda

2 tsp. cream of tartar

1 cup sour cream

7 cups flour

Instructions:

1. Cream together the sugar, lard, and eggs.

2. Mix baking soda, cream of tartar, and sour cream together. Add alternately with flour to the creamed mixture.

3. Refrigerate overnight or for several hours. Roll out dough and cut in desired shapes. Bake at 400°F for 8–10 minutes.

SUGAR COOKIES FOR A CROWD

Makes about 9 dozen cookies.

Ingredients:
4½ cups brown sugar
2 cups lard, melted
2 cups sour cream
8 eggs
3 tsp. soda
3 tsp. cream of tartar
9 cups flour
1 Tbsp. vanilla
Pinch of salt

Instructions:
1. Cream the sugar and lard. Add the sour cream and eggs and beat well. Stir in the remaining ingredients and mix well.

2. Drop by teaspoonsful onto greased cookie sheets. Bake at 325°F for 8–10 minutes.

Recipe Notes: The Amish expect unannounced company. They are seldom caught unprepared with their bountifully stocked canning shelves and flourishing gardens.

One efficient and experienced cook has found a way to both entertain and feed her guests. "I mix a big batch of sugar cookies and only bake half of them at a time. The other half I keep in the refrigerator for up to two to three weeks. What I like is if someone comes, then you have something to do. And the cookies are much better, too, when they're fresh!"

MOLASSES COOKIES

Makes 8 dozen cookies.

Ingredients:

1 cup butter or margarine
½ lb. light brown sugar
1 pint dark baking molasses
1 pint buttermilk
6 cups flour
1 Tbsp. baking soda

Instructions:

1. Cream butter and sugar. Add molasses and buttermilk.

2. Stir in flour and baking soda.

3. Drop in large dollops from teaspoon onto cookie sheet. Bake at 375°F for 8–10 minutes.

Recipe Notes: Molasses cookies, along with sugar cookies, top the list of fondly remembered old favorites. Molasses was a commonly used sweetener in the 19th century when refined sugar was at a premium in the New World.

Today's molasses cookies also call for sugar, but they retain the sturdy, cakey quality that has always made them loved.

Variations abound from household to household.

"We ate molasses spice."

"Ours were fat molasses cookies."

"We had soft molasses cakes with icing."

Variations:

• Cookies may be glazed by brushing tops with egg yolks before baking.

• Add 1 tsp. ginger and 1 tsp. cinnamon with flour and sugar.

ROLLED OATS COOKIES

Makes 9 dozen cookies.

Ingredients:

2 cups brown sugar

1 cup lard or vegetable shortening

3 eggs

1 cup sour milk or buttermilk

1 tsp. vanilla

3 cups flour

1 tsp. baking powder

1 tsp. baking soda

1 tsp. cinnamon

½ tsp. nutmeg

½ tsp. salt

2 cups rolled oats

2 cups raisins

1 cup nuts, chopped

Instructions:

1. Cream together the sugar, lard, eggs, milk, and vanilla.

2. Stir dry ingredients together.

3. Combine dry ingredients with creamed mixture, blending thoroughly.

4. Drop by teaspoonsful onto greased cookie sheets. Bake at 350°F for 12–15 minutes.

Recipe Notes: "Next to molasses and sugar cookies we ate oatmeal cookies. We always bought oatmeal by the 50-pound bag."

BUTTERSCOTCH COOKIES

Makes 7–8 dozen cookies.

Ingredients:
2 cups brown sugar
3 eggs
1 cup shortening or lard
4 cups flour
1 tsp. baking soda
1 tsp. cream of tartar
1 cup nuts

Instructions:
1. Mix all ingredients but the nuts thoroughly in a mixer. Stir the nuts in by hand.

2. Roll the dough into ropes about 2 inches thick. Cut in thin slices. Cross-press with a fork to make a design.

3. Bake at 350°F for 8–12 minutes.

SOUR CREAM COOKIES

Makes 12–13 dozen cookies.

Ingredients:

3 cups granulated sugar
1¾ cups lard or shortening
4 eggs
1 cup sour milk
1 cup sour cream
2 tsp. baking soda
4 tsp. baking powder
¾ tsp. salt
6 cups flour
1 tsp. lemon flavoring
1 Tbsp. vanilla

Instructions:

1. Cream together sugar, lard, and eggs.

2. Mix in remaining ingredients, combining thoroughly.

3. Roll out and cut in desired shapes. Sprinkle tops with granulated sugar.

4. Bake on greased cookie sheets at 350°F for 8–10 minutes.

BUTTERMILK COOKIES

Makes 9 dozen cookies.

Ingredients:

2 cups brown sugar

1 cup lard or vegetable shortening

1 tsp. vanilla

2 eggs

2 tsp. baking soda

1 cup buttermilk

2 tsp. baking powder

4 cups flour

½ cup nuts, chopped (optional)

Instructions:

1. Cream together sugar and lard. Mix in vanilla and eggs thoroughly.

2. Dissolve baking soda in buttermilk.

3. Stir baking powder into flour.

4. Add milk and flour mixture alternately to the creamed mixture. Stir in nuts.

5. Refrigerate overnight or for several hours. Drop by teaspoonsful onto greased cookie sheet. Bake at 400°F for 8–10 minutes.

HERMITS

Makes about 10 dozen cookies.

Ingredients:

1 cup shortening

1 cup granulated sugar

1 cup brown sugar

4 eggs

½ cup molasses

1 tsp. baking soda dissolved in ½ cup warm water

4½ cups flour

¼ tsp. salt

¼ tsp. ground cloves

1 cup chopped nuts

1 cup chopped dates

Instructions:

1. Cream shortening and sugars. Add eggs and beat until light and fluffy.

2. Sift dry ingredients and add alternately with water–and–baking soda mixture and molasses. Beat after each addition.

3. Stir in chopped nuts and dates.

4. Drop by round teaspoons onto greased cookie sheet. Bake at 350°F for 10–12 minutes.

Recipe Notes: Many varieties of dried fruit and nut cookies filled the farm pantries. Chewy and substantial, they also retained their moisture longer because of the presence of the fruit.

Here are hermits, those old-fashioned cousins of jumbies, ice box cookies, date and nut, and mincemeat cookies.

Variations:

- Use ½ cup cooled black coffee instead of water.

- Add 1 cup raisins and 1 cup chopped dried apricots in place of nuts and dates.

GINGER COOKIES

Makes 9–10 dozen cookies.

Ingredients:

1 cup lard, butter, or margarine
1 cup granulated sugar
1 egg
2 cups dark baking molasses
2 Tbsp. vinegar
6–8 cups flour
¾ tsp. salt
½ tsp. cinnamon
2 Tbsp. ginger
4 tsp. baking soda
1 cup boiling water

Instructions:

1. Cream together lard, sugar, and egg. When light and fluffy beat in molasses and vinegar.

2. Stir together dry ingredients.

3. Dissolve baking soda in boiling water.

4. Add dry ingredients and mixture of baking soda and water alternately to creamed ingredients. Add more flour if needed to make a soft dough.

5. Drop by teaspoonsful onto greased cookie sheets. Sprinkle with granulated sugar. Bake at 350°F for 10 minutes.

PINWHEEL DATE COOKIES

Makes 3½ dozen cookies.

Ingredients:
1 cup shortening
2 cups brown sugar
½ cup granulated sugar
3 eggs
4–4½ cups flour
1 tsp. salt
1 tsp. baking soda
1 tsp. cinnamon

Instructions:
1. Cream together the shortening and sugars. Add the eggs and beat until fluffy.

2. Sift the flour; then add the salt, baking soda, and cinnamon and sift again. Add the dry ingredients to the creamed mixture and beat until smooth.

3. Chill dough in the refrigerator for a few hours. Divide the chilled dough into two parts. Roll each ¼ inch thick and spread with filling (recipe below).

Recipe Notes: This cookie was not part of the weekly baking; it requires far too much time in preparation! But it has traditionally been part of holiday cookie-making.

Filling
1½ cups dates or raisins, ground
1 cup sugar
1 cup water
½ cup nuts, chopped fine

Instructions:
1. Combine the fruit, sugar, and water and cook until thickened, stirring constantly. Remove from heat and add the nuts. Cool and spread on the rolled dough.

2. Roll up, jelly-roll fashion, and chill thoroughly in the refrigerator. Slice the rings ⅛ inch thick and place on greased cookie sheets, 1 inch apart. Bake at 375°F until golden brown.

RAISIN-FILLED COOKIES

Makes 5–6 dozen cookies.

Ingredients:

1 cup lard or vegetable shortening
2 cups granulated sugar
2 eggs, beaten
1 cup milk
2 tsp. vanilla
7 cups flour
2 tsp. baking soda
2 tsp. baking powder

Filling

2 cups raisins, chopped or ground
1 cup sugar
1 cup water
2 Tbsp. flour
1 Tbsp. lemon juice (optional)

Instructions:

1. Cream lard, sugar, and eggs together. Blend eggs and milk. Combine with creamed mixture. Add vanilla.

2. Sift together dry ingredients and mix well. Stir thoroughly into batter.

3. Chill dough in the refrigerator for several hours or overnight. Roll to ¼-inch thickness on lightly floured board. Cut out with round cutter.

4. To make the filling, combine all ingredients and bring to a boil, stirring constantly until thickened.

5. Place 1 teaspoon of raisin filling on the top of each of half the cookies.

6. With a thimble make a hole in the middle of the remaining cookies (the hole will prevent the filling from cooking out between the cookie halves). Place these cookies on top of the cookies with filling. Do not press together.

7. Bake at 350°F for 20 minutes on greased cookie sheets.

SAND TARTS

Makes 4–5 dozen cookies.

Ingredients:

1 cup butter
2 cups granulated sugar
3 eggs
1 tsp. vanilla
1 tsp. salt
2 tsp. baking powder
3½–4 cups flour

Instructions:

1. Cream together butter and sugar. Add eggs and vanilla and beat until fluffy.

2. Mix dry ingredients together and beat into batter until a soft dough forms. Refrigerate several hours or overnight.

3. Roll dough very thin and cut in decorative shapes with cookie cutters. Brush tops of cookies with egg whites and sprinkle with colored sugar and crushed peanuts, walnuts, or pecans.

4. Bake at 350°F for 8–10 minutes on greased cookie sheets.

Recipe Notes: Although Christmas is celebrated quietly, some families have kept a few cooking traditions, especially to honor visitors over the holidays.

At the turn of the century, sand tarts were baked in some homes "at Christmastime, and usually only then. We would cut them out in different shapes," an elderly woman remarks. The traditional Pennsylvania Dutch Cookies—*lebkuchen, pfefferniss,* and *springerle*—were not commonly eaten by the Amish. Explained an Amish grandfather, "We had more cookies around at Christmas, but not really special kinds."

Today cookie-baking is associated more with holiday activity, and sand tarts continue as favorites, perhaps because children enjoy both cutting them out and choosing special shapes to eat.

WHOOPIE PIES

Makes 4 dozen sandwich pies.

Ingredients:

2 cups sugar

1 cup shortening

2 eggs

4 cups flour

1 cup baking cocoa

1 tsp. salt

1 cup sour milk

2 tsp. vanilla

2 tsp. baking soda

1 cup hot water

Instructions:

1. Cream sugar and shortening. Add eggs.

2. Sift together flour, cocoa, and salt. Add to creamed mixture alternately with sour milk. Add vanilla.

3. Dissolve baking soda in hot water and add last. Mix well.

4. Drop by rounded teaspoonful onto cookie sheet. Bake at 400°F for 8–10 minutes.

5. Make sandwiches from 2 cookies filled with Whoopie Pie Filling (recipe below).

Recipe Notes: These cookies are a relatively new invention, first appearing about 30–35 years ago. Said one grandmother in her mid-50s, "I don't remember whoopie pies as a little girl, but I do know they were around before we were married. Probably someone just made them up!"

Another grandmother in her late 50s knew of them "just since we're married, and that not in the first years."

These individual cakes are well suited to lunch-box travel and food stands at farm sales. The icing is spread between the two cookie halves so it doesn't rub off when wrapped, as cupcake icing does.

The original—and still most commonly made—whoopie pie is chocolate. Oatmeal and pumpkin variations have developed more recently.

Filling

2 egg whites, beaten

4 Tbsp. milk

2 tsp. vanilla

4 cups confectioners' sugar

1½ cups shortening

Instructions:

1. Mix together egg whites, milk, vanilla, and 2 cups confectioners' sugar. Then beat in shortening and remaining 2 cups of confectioners' sugar.

2. Spread dab of filling on flat side of cooled cookie. Top with another cookie to form a sandwich pie.

OATMEAL WHOOPIE PIES

Makes 3 dozen sandwich pies.

Ingredients:

2 cups brown sugar
¾ cup butter
2 eggs
½ tsp. salt
1 tsp. cinnamon
1 tsp. baking powder
1 tsp. baking soda
3 Tbsp. boiling water
2½ cups flour
2 cups oatmeal

Instructions:

1. Cream sugar and butter. Add eggs; then add salt, cinnamon, and baking powder.

2. Add baking soda dissolved in hot water. Gradually add flour and oatmeal.

3. Drop batter by heaping teaspoons onto greased cookie sheet. Bake at 350°F for 8–10 minutes or until brown.

4. Use ½ recipe Whoopie Pie Filling (page 125) to fill sandwich pies.

PUMPKIN WHOOPIE PIES

Makes 3 dozen sandwich pies.

Ingredients:

2 cups brown sugar

1 cup vegetable oil

1½ cups cooked, mashed pumpkin

2 eggs

3 cups flour

1 tsp. salt

1 tsp. baking powder

1 tsp. baking soda

1 tsp. vanilla

1½ Tbsp. cinnamon

½ Tbsp. ginger

½ Tbsp. ground cloves

Instructions:

1. Cream sugar and oil.

2. Add pumpkin and eggs. Add flour, salt, baking powder, baking soda, vanilla, and spices. Mix well.

3. Drop by heaping teaspoons onto greased cookie sheet. Bake at 350°F for 10–12 minutes.

4. Make sandwiches from 2 cookies filled with ½ recipe Whoopie Pie Filling (page 125).

Variation:

Adding ½ cup black walnuts (ground) gives these cookies a special delicious flavor.

CONVERSION CHARTS

METRIC AND IMPERIAL CONVERSIONS

(These conversions are rounded for convenience)

Ingredient	Cups/Tablespoons/ Teaspoons	Ounces	Grams/Milliliters
Butter	1 cup/ 16 tablespoons/ 2 sticks	8 ounces	230 grams
Cheese, shredded	1 cup	4 ounces	110 grams
Cream cheese	1 tablespoon	0.5 ounce	14.5 grams
Cornstarch	1 tablespoon	0.3 ounce	8 grams
Flour, all-purpose	1 cup/1 tablespoon	4.5 ounces/0.3 ounce	125 grams/8 grams
Flour, whole wheat	1 cup	4 ounces	120 grams
Fruit, dried	1 cup	4 ounces	120 grams
Fruits or veggies, chopped	1 cup	5 to 7 ounces	145 to 200 grams
Fruits or veggies, pureed	1 cup	8.5 ounces	245 grams
Honey, maple syrup, or corn syrup	1 tablespoon	0.75 ounce	20 grams
Liquids: cream, milk, water, or juice	1 cup	8 fluid ounces	240 milliliters
Oats	1 cup	5.5 ounces	150 grams
Salt	1 teaspoon	0.2 ounce	6 grams
Spices: cinnamon, cloves, ginger, or nutmeg (ground)	1 teaspoon	0.2 ounce	5 milliliters
Sugar, brown, firmly packed	1 cup	7 ounces	200 grams
Sugar, white	1 cup/1 tablespoon	7 ounces/0.5 ounce	200 grams/12.5 grams
Vanilla extract	1 teaspoon	0.2 ounce	4 grams

OVEN TEMPERATURES

Fahrenheit	Celsius	Gas Mark
225°	110°	¼
250°	120°	½
275°	140°	1
300°	150°	2
325°	160°	3
350°	180°	4
375°	190°	5
400°	200°	6
425°	220°	7
450°	230°	8

INDEX

NOTES

NOTES

NOTES

NOTES

NOTES

··

··

··

··

··

··

··

··

··

··

··

··

··

··

··

··

NOTES

NOTES

··

··

··

··

··

··

··

··

··

··

··

··

··

··

··

NOTES

NOTES

NOTES

··

··

··

··

··

··

··

··

··

··

··

··

··

··

··

NOTES

NOTES

NOTES

NOTES

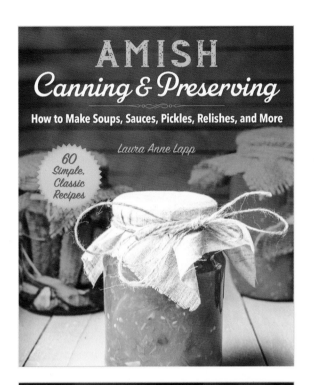

AMISH
Canning & Preserving
How to Make Soups, Sauces, Pickles, Relishes, and More

Laura Anne Lapp

60 Simple, Classic Recipes

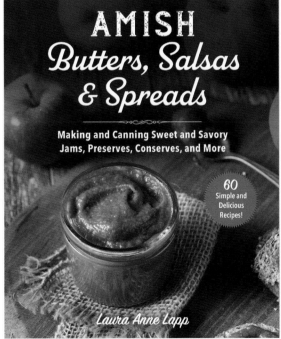

AMISH
Butters, Salsas & Spreads
Making and Canning Sweet and Savory
Jams, Preserves, Conserves, and More

60 Simple and Delicious Recipes!

Laura Anne Lapp